The Butterfly amongst the Bees

RUBEI NIKKOL

ISBN: 978-1-968061-13-5

This story is more than a tale of a butterfly and some bees—
It is a reflection of the journey many of us face:
The desire to belong, the pain of rejection, and the quiet courage to rise again.

The Butterfly amongst the Bees was born from a place of deep faith, love, and purpose. Inspired by moments of stillness, whispered prayers, and the beauty of transformation, this story invites readers—both young and old—to recognize the masterpiece that lives within them.

Sarah, the little butterfly, reminds us that even in the face of fear or judgment, we are not alone. There is a wind that carries us, a voice that gently calls us to shine, and a place of harmony waiting when we choose forgiveness, love, and unity.

I pray this book brings comfort to the hurting, hope to the lonely, and light to those who feel unseen.

Let this be a gentle reminder:
You are seen.
You are loved.
You were created with intention.

With grace and gratitude,
RUBEI NIKKOL

The Lord is my Shepherd,
I shall not want.

Psalms 23:1

I believe this book to be a truly inspired word of GOD.

- RUBEI NIKKOL

In dedication to Sarah,
our beloved family
and the Heavens above

In loving Memory
Of
Marissa Babe

" That, I shall always seek you,
and, find the good in others"

In the beginning,
God created, the sun, the moon, the stars,
the flowers and the trees,

He also created,

Butterflies and Bees...

And, so it was told,
that there would be a story to behold,
about a little butterfly who was bullied by
the bees...

"The Butterfly amongst the Bees"

By: RUBEI NIKKOL

An array of beautiful scents filled the air, and the tree leaves blew with the winds, now this attracted the butterflies and the bees, and even hummingbirds and other such things.

Now, the bees,
they traveled in swarms,
and enjoyed the summer's warmth.
The growth of new flowers and trees,
tickled their little feet.
They'd play in the fields each day,
They'd frolic around, and spend the day in
the hot summer's rays.

Meanwhile,
somewhere far away,

a butterfly, named Sarah, was coming out to play.

She'd spent weeks transforming
from a caterpillar
into the butterfly,
she had aspired to be.

Sarah's wings were Big and Bright, and her colors were Bold, they were all the colors of the rainbow!

Sarah was exceptionally social and oh-so sweet,
She was quite different and extraordinarily unique.

She loved to spread her colorful wings and fly,
She loved to flutter around and get lost in the midst of the sky.

She loved all the flowers and the trees,
but, most of all, she loved the summer's breeze.

however,

the bees,

They would chase her out of the garden and into
the trees, they'd buzz so loudly in her ear, they'd
frighten her so much, that it would cause her fear!
This made her feel scared, sad, and alone,
She didn't have one friend to call her own.
She would hide in the trees, away from the bees
and even though her colors shone so bright,
She tucked them in and hid from the light.

The small little butterfly, no longer flew in the skies,
she didn't spread her wings to fly,
and she no longer flew out at sunrise.

Instead, she stayed in the trees,
and hid from the bees.

She did not talk, or try and play,
instead she huddled in sadness and disarray.

Then,
suddenly one day,
the wind came and whispered in her ear and said,

"Sarah come out and play.",

and

took her by the hand and carried her away.

and,
although she was frightened of the bees,
the wind carried her beneath and above the trees
and said,

"Please do not be afraid of me".

"Sarah", it softly spoke...

"Seek me in the light and I will find you even in the night."

"I will be your shield and your protector,
I will always be here for you,
this, I promise to you always and forever".

"So please be bold, and please be kind,
be unique and show your shine,
you are perfect in every way,
you are my masterpiece, by the way".

"And please be strong and persevere,
through all the Big and Little fears."

"Do not let anything or anyone hold you down,
you are my little angel, so please do not frown".

The wind then carried her,
thru the dandelions, daylilies, and rose bushes,
and across the bluest skies,

it swept her above the ocean tides.

And when the day was gone, it nestled her in the fields, and as she slept, it whispered in her ear,

"You are an Image of me,
And everything I intended you to be."

As,
daylight broke,
the little bees awoke.
"Hooray, it's time to play!",
as a bird flew across their way.

The bird softly spoke,
and the bees were frightened as can be,
utter shock and disbelief.

"My little children, please do not be afraid of me."
"Do not anger and do not be mean,
do not be quick to be unkeen."

"Do not judge me for who I am,
judge me fairly, as would I,
because not all actions are justified".

"My little children,
there is a story to be told,
a story yet to unfold."

"So, please be kind, and
Please do not leave broken hearts behind."
"And so, I say, let's all go play and enjoy this wonderful day!"

Sarah remembered everything said,
as she flew out and kissed the flower beds.

The bees, then came with loving hearts,
and asked for forgiveness and a brand-new start.

"Sarah,

We promise not to frown upon you,

but to be caring and kind,

and keep you in mind,

every time we come out and play in the sunshine."

Sarah, then said,

"I promise to be a good friend,
and do all I can,

to always be there with an open heart,
and a helping hand."

You see,
they had a common purpose,
to be in harmony,

as one,
all under the bright yellow sun.

With all the love that they would sow,

That love would help the flowers to grow.

And,

that's how,

the butterfly and the bees,

came to be

to come together,

and pollinate,

the flowers and the trees.

For every season,

There is a reason,

To find a new way,

And make a change,

For the better and the good,

What is for the best

Will be understood.

So,

Follow your heart,

And follow the path,

Follow the rainbow,

That you shall hath.

- RUBEI NIKKOL

Let The Butterfly amongst the Bees be more than just
a story—
Let it be a movement.

Let us teach our children to embrace one another's
differences.
Let us model kindness, even when it's hard.
Let us speak up for those who feel silenced.
Let us create spaces where every "Sarah" can shine.

Whether in our homes, our schools, or our
communities,
May we choose compassion over criticism,
Acceptance over exclusion,
And love over fear.

Be the wind that lifts someone.

Be the voice that brings peace.

Be the heart that helps the garden grow.

Now, go out and pollinate the world—with kindness.

www.ingramcontent.com/pod-product-compliance
Lightning Source LLC
Chambersburg PA
CBHW080425030426
42335CB00020B/2598